Cambridge **Discovery Education**™

►**INTERACTIVE READERS**

Series editor: Bob Hastings

YOUR DREAM
VACATION

A1+

Susan Evento

CAMBRIDGE UNIVERSITY PRESS
Cambridge, New York, Melbourne, Madrid, Cape Town,
Singapore, São Paulo, Delhi, Mexico City

Cambridge University Press
32 Avenue of the Americas, New York, NY 10013-2473, USA

www.cambridge.org
Information on this title: www.cambridge.org/9781107690431

First published 2014

Printed in Hong Kong, China, by Golden Cup Printing Company Limited

A catalog record for this publication is available from the British Library.

Library of Congress Cataloging-in-Publication Data

Evento, Susan.
  Your dream vacation / Susan Evento.
    pages cm. -- (Cambridge discovery interactive readers)
  ISBN 978-1-107-69043-1 (pbk. : alk. paper)
  1. Vacations--Juvenile literature. 2. English language--Textbooks for foreign speakers.
  3. Readers (Elementary) I. Title.

LB3041.E84 2013
790.083--dc23

                          2013025116

ISBN 978-1-107-69043-1

Additional resources for this publication at www.cambridge.org

Layout services, art direction, book design, and photo research: Q2ABillSMITH GROUP
Editorial services: Hyphen S.A.
Audio production: CityVox, New York
Video production: Q2ABillSMITH GROUP

Contents

Before You Read:
Get Ready!

There are many different kinds of vacations. You can travel or stay at home. You can visit unusual places or have fun in the sun or the snow. What's your "dream vacation"?

Words to Know

Look at the pictures. Then complete the sentences below with the correct words.

desert

forest

festival

island

lake

mountains

1 People take a boat to get to the _____ .

2 At a _____ there is often music and dancing.

3 The highest _____ in the world are in the Himalayas.

4 I like trees a lot, so I like to walk in the _____ .

5 We needed water in the hot _____ .

6 Let's go for a swim in the _____ .

Words to Know

Read the paragraph. Then complete the definitions below with the correct highlighted words.

What is your dream vacation? Some people like to go places where they have peace and quiet. They go on spa vacations where they get to relax and feel wonderful. But my dream vacation is one with lots of activities! I like hiking in the mountains, swimming, horse riding, and taking boat rides. Every year I go to a great summer camp where I can do all these things. And in the winter I like skiing down the snowy mountains.

1 _____ : not work, not be busy or worried

2 _____ : things you do, like playing baseball

3 _____ : a feeling you get when it is quiet

4 _____ : a winter sport

5 _____ : a type of vacation you want a lot

6 _____ : very good

7 _____ : walking for fun or sport

Kids can do lots of different activities at summer camp.

CHAPTER 1

Time to Play

SO YOU'RE READY FOR A VACATION. WHERE SHOULD YOU GO, AND WHAT SHOULD YOU DO?

Put a check (✓) next to things that are important to you.

_____ traveling **far** away

_____ being near water

_____ seeing something new

_____ going back to a favorite place

_____ being with friends

_____ being with family

_____ having "me time"

_____ doing lots of activities

_____ going somewhere warm

_____ learning something new

Let's look at a few dream vacations.

Raúl is on an airplane. Where is he going? Home! He lives in Chile, far away from his family in New York. The last time he saw them was more than a year ago. He can't wait to be with them.

Sabine is on a **tour** with a group of people. They are at the Louvre Museum in Paris. A **guide** is telling them about the paintings. This is one stop on Sabine's vacation to learn about art in Europe.

Carmen is in the middle of a river in fast water. What is she doing? White water rafting in Turkey! Carmen goes somewhere new each year where she can get better at her favorite sport.

Maybe these aren't your dream vacations. But dream vacations aren't the same for everyone. It's time to find *your* dream vacation!

?

APPLY

What was your last vacation? Did you enjoy it? Was it a dream vacation? Why or why not?

White water rafting

CHAPTER 2

Relaxing Vacations

WANT TO RELAX AND HAVE A QUIET TIME? MAYBE THESE VACATIONS ARE FOR YOU.

A white sand beach on Koh Lipe

You need to leave your computer at home and your cell phone off for this vacation in Thailand.

Koh Lipe is a small island in the Andaman Sea. You can only get there by boat. There aren't any cars on the island. There aren't any banks, either, so bring money. But you don't need to bring much. It's not expensive. You can stay in some places for only $20 a night.

There are four beautiful beaches with white sand. You can go snorkeling in beautiful blue water.

Snorkeling

You can relax with a massage.

Yoga can also help you to relax.

The Vigilius Mountain **Resort** is in Lana, Italy. Here, at 1,500 meters, you're in your own "island" in the mountains.

There aren't any roads, so you need to take a cable car[1] to get there. There *is* a lot of peace and quiet, and a beautiful **view** of the Dolomite Mountains.

You can get a massage at the spa, swim in the pool, and take yoga classes. In the winter, you can also go skiing.

....

[1]**cable car:** a kind of train that goes up a mountain

Video Quest

Relaxing in Tuscany

Watch this video to learn about other ways to relax in Italy. What does the Percalese family do?

This hotel has great views of the mountains.

People on a snowmobile tour of Lake Louise.

In the Canadian Rocky Mountains, you can stay at the Fairmont Chateau Hotel. This beautiful hotel has great views of Lake Louise and the mountains. It has a relaxing spa, too. But there are also lots of activities you can do, including hiking, skiing, and snowmobiling.

These places are relaxing, but traveling can be a lot of work. Sometimes when you're stressed[2] from school and work, you don't want to **plan** a vacation. You don't want to **pack** and travel. Sometimes, the most relaxing vacation is staying at home – a "staycation."

[2] **stressed:** worried because of too much work

Get comfortable on the couch. Watch movies and read books. Or maybe you want to relax doing a favorite hobby.[3]

On your staycation, maybe you want to take short **trips** to places near you, enjoy the beach, have a picnic in the park, or visit your favorite museum. It's nice to spend time with family and friends, too.

Maybe the best staycation is to give yourself a gift. Pay someone to clean your house, wash your clothes, and cook for you. Or call your favorite restaurants and pay them to send food to your house. It's like being in a hotel.

[3]**hobby:** something you do for fun when you're not working

Do you like to get comfortable on the couch?

A rodeo

CHAPTER 3

Active Vacations

**SOME VACATIONS ARE ALL ABOUT ACTIVITIES –
DO YOUR FAVORITE THINGS OR TRY NEW THINGS.**

They're cooking dinner over a campfire. Someone says, "Come and get it!" Where are you? On vacation at a dude ranch in Colorado!

If you want to ride horses and feel like a cowboy, then this is your dream vacation. There's no better way to see the American West than riding a horse along a trail.[4]

At dude ranches you can also be in a rodeo! Or you can get off the horse and do other activities, like hiking or fishing. And in some places you can go white water rafting or skiing, too.

[4]**trail:** a road for horses

Video Quest

Fun in the Snow

Watch this video about winter activities in Montana, USA. What sports are these people enjoying?

Maybe the life of a rock star, not a cowboy, is for you. If so, you can go on vacation to a Rock 'n' Roll Fantasy Camp. There are camps in the USA, England, and the Bahamas.

You play, write, and record music in a studio with famous musicians like Steven Tyler of Aerosmith or Nick Mason of Pink Floyd. At the end, you play on stage.[5] And you can get on TV. Rock 'n' Roll Fantasy Camp is now a TV show.

[5] **stage:** something higher than the floor that musicians play on

Musicians playing together on stage

Peace and love. It's the Love Parade!

This festival began in East Berlin just months before the Berlin Wall came down in 1989. It was a festival for world peace and understanding – and to enjoy electronic music.[6] Now many cities in different places in the world have Love Parade festivals: Budapest, Hungary; Sydney, Australia; Santiago, Chile.

What happens at a Love Parade? There's a lot of dancing. DJs from around the world travel on floats and play electronic music. People at the festival dance all day and night. It's great fun, but you can get really tired.

6 **electronic music:** music made by computers

DJs on floats play music.

The Rio Carnival has colorful costumes and parade floats.

?

APPLY

What are your favorite activities? Where would you go on vacation to enjoy them?

Or take a vacation to the beautiful South American city of Rio de Janeiro, in Brazil – the home of the 2016 Olympics. It's the first South American city to have the Olympics.

It's also the home of the biggest Carnival festival in the world. People from many countries go there for Carnival. It's a four-day national holiday with street parties, parades with colorful floats, and people wearing wonderful costumes. And lots of Brazilian samba: music, singing, and dancing!

A penguin

CHAPTER 4

Exotic Vacations

MAYBE YOU PREFER BEAUTIFUL AND UNUSUAL VACATIONS IN INTERESTING, FARAWAY PLACES.

Do you want to visit exotic places? Why not take a vacation at the end of the world?

Ushuaia, in Argentina, is the world's most southern city. It's closer to Antarctica than it is to Buenos Aires. Ushuaia has lakes, forests, glaciers, beautiful rainbows, and the Andes Mountains. So you can fish, hike, and ski. And if you take a boat ride, you can see penguins up close.

A glacier

There are many wonderful places in **nature**, but there are only seven **Natural** Wonders of the World. Victoria Falls in southern Africa, on the Zambezi River, is one of them. It's the largest waterfall in the world. You can hear it long before you see it – 935 cubic meters of water fall every second! It's really noisy!

Be sure to visit the Falls between late November and late April, when it doesn't rain so much. You can see and do more then. You can swim in "The Devil's Swimming Pool" on the edge of the Falls. Or you can see a beautiful moonbow – a rainbow made by the light of a full moon through the water of the Falls.

The Devil's Swimming Pool is on the edge of the waterfall.

The full moon makes a rainbow at Victoria Falls.

Video Quest

A Trip Through the Sahara

Watch this video to learn about life in Morocco in the Sahara Desert. How is life in Morocco unusual?

Do you want to see more of nature's wonders? Go to Uluru in central Australia. It isn't one of the Seven Natural Wonders, but it is wonderful.

Uluru is a very big rock. It's 348 meters tall and over 9 kilometers around. It's also very old – 500 million years! The Aborigines, the first people of Australia, tell stories about it. They say their ancestors[7] made it. You can go on a tour with a guide to learn why Uluru is so important to the Aborigines.

You can stay in a hotel, or you can camp. Eat in an outdoor restaurant at sunset and watch the wonderful changing colors of beautiful Uluru.

[7]**ancestors:** people in your family that lived a long time ago

Sunset at Uluru

The host of *Jeopardy* talks to the audience before the show begins.

Do you like watching TV? Well, how about taking a vacation where you can be in the audience of a TV show? *Jeopardy* is a popular TV quiz show in the USA. People try to answer questions for money.

They make *Jeopardy* near Hollywood, which is famous, of course, as the home of movies. You can be in the audience of a TV show, see where movie stars live, and visit Universal Studios or Disneyland!

APPLY

Which one would you like to do – visit Uluru or be in the audience of a TV show? Why?

CHAPTER 5

What Do You Think?

WHICH DREAM VACATION IS FOR YOU?

Look at these vacations. Put a 1 next to those you don't find interesting, a 2 next to those that are interesting to you, and a 3 next to those you would really like.

_____ Koh Lipe island in Thailand

_____ The Vigilius Mountain Resort in Lana, Italy

_____ Tuscany, Italy

_____ The Fairmont Chateau Hotel on Lake Louise

_____ A staycation

_____ A dude ranch in Colorado

_____ Rock 'n' Roll Fantasy Camp in London, England

_____ Snowboarding and skiing in Montana

_____ The Love Parade Festival in Santiago, Chile

_____ Ushuaia, Argentina

_____ Victoria Falls in Africa

_____ Morocco, North Africa

_____ A TV show audience in Hollywood

Which ones did you give a 1? What is the same about all of them – the place, the weather, activities, nature, natural wonders?

How many 3's did you give? Did you find your dream vacation in this book? What is your dream vacation?

Remember, for a great vacation, you need to plan. Read about places on the Internet. Talk to friends about their vacations. Choose how to get there. Choose where to stay. Then start dreaming about all the fun you're going to have. And get ready to pack your bags.

Of course, if you want a staycation, it's easier. Just get those books and movies ready!

Enjoy your dream vacation!

After You Read

True or False

Circle True or False for each sentence.

1. A guide takes people on a tour of places.   True   False
2. Koh Lipe is a mountain.   True   False
3. Lake Louise is in northern Italy.   True   False
4. You don't have to pack or travel to take a staycation.   True   False
5. A dude ranch is somewhere you go to ride horses.   True   False
6. The Love Parade Festival began in Santiago, Chile, in 1989.   True   False
7. There is a famous carnival in Rio.   True   False

Complete the Sentences

Use the words in the box to complete the sentences.

guide	pack	plan	tour	trip	view

1. Our _____ to the museum was fun.
2. There is a beautiful _____ of the mountains from the Fairmont Chateau Hotel.
3. Our _____ knows a lot about this city.
4. We took a _____ of the Louvre museum in Paris.
5. I don't need to bring many clothes for a beach vacation. It will be easy to _____.
6. It's a lot of work to _____ a vacation. Let's take a staycation this year.

Where Am I?

Match the places with the correct locations.

1 _____ Uluru   **a** northern Italy

2 _____ Victoria Falls   **b** the Rocky Mountains

3 _____ Koh Lipe   **c** central Australia

4 _____ Ushuaia   **d** southwestern Thailand

5 _____ The Vigilius Mountain Resort   **e** southern Argentina

6 _____ The Fairmont Chateau Hotel   **f** southern Africa

Choosing a Vacation

Choose three vacations from this book. Where are they?
Write down one good thing and one bad thing about
each vacation.

Where is it?	What's good?	What's bad?
1.		
2.		
3.		

Answer Key

Words to Know, page 4
1 island **2** festival **3** mountains **4** forest **5** desert
6 lake

Words to Know, page 5
1 relax **2** activities **3** peace **4** skiing
5 dream vacation **6** wonderful **7** hiking

Apply, page 7   *Answers will vary.*

Video Quest, page 9
They run a family restaurant, a trattoria.

Video Quest, page 13
Snowboarding and skiing.

Apply, page 15   *Answers will vary.*

Video Quest, page 17
Life in the desert is the same now as it was hundreds of years ago.

Apply, page 19   *Answers will vary.*

True or False?, page 22
1 True **2** False **3** False **4** True **5** True **6** False **7** True

Complete the Sentences, page 22
1 trip **2** view **3** guide **4** tour **5** pack **6** plan

Where Am I?, page 23
1 c **2** f **3** d **4** e **5** a **6** b

Choosing a Vacation, page 23   *Answers will vary.*